Some Aspects of Dinka Noun System

Deng Akol Juach

PhD, Language and Linguistics

© Deng Akol Juach, 2020

ISBN: 978-0-6487937-9-3

All rights reserved. No part of this publication may be reproduced, stored in a retrieval system, or transmitted, in any form, or by any means, electronic, mechanical, photocopying, recording or otherwise, without the prior permission of the publishers.

This book is sold subject to the conditions that it shall not, by way of trade or otherwise, be lent, re-sold, hired out or otherwise circulated without the publisher's prior consent in any form of binding or cover other than in which it is published and without a similar condition including the condition being imposed on the subsequent purchaser.

Africa World Books Pty. Ltd.

Design and typesetting: Africa World Books

Dedication

This book is dedicated to the loving memory of my parents, Akol Juach and Apat Dut Jok

Acknowledgements

I want to thank the following colleagues and friends for the technical advice and encouragement they offered to me. My thanks go to Atem Yaak Atem, a long-term editorial consultant, who took the responsibility of stylistic and copy editing of the text and for making relevant adjustments to Dinka words, phrases and sentences with special reference to the application of "breathy" vowels and "non-breathy" vowels. I thank Professor Mairi Blackings of the University of Juba for his untiring efforts he made to improve this book by way of intervention in technical aspects of the work. I am also grateful to Professor Marop Leek for introducing me to Professor Taban lo Liyong who in turn arranged my meeting with Professor Blackings, a contact that has blossomed into fruitful working relationship and friendship as shown by this book.

Preface

The Government of South Sudan's policy towards the development of national and local languages has necessitated publication of this book. Also, the fact that Dinka is one of the major Nilotic languages and it lagged behind in the field of linguistics, especially in phonology, morphology, syntax and semantics raises the morphological work. The objective of this book is to help those interested and desire to learn how to read and write in Dinka language with the intention of having linguistic background. The book is very straightforward in the introduction of Dinka historical background, social background, the distribution of the Dinka people in South Sudan and in the contested Abyei region of South Kordofan, and review of literature of the Dinka as a language.

The book also reiterates on the Dinka phonology and discusses the presence of both "hard" and "breathy" voice in the pronunciation of vowels, diphthongs and semi-vowels. Tone, vowel system and syllable are included in the discussion. Furthermore, compounding, word-formation, cattle name prefixes and reduplication are tackled in chapter four and chapter five respectively.

Without forgetting, I am grateful to Mrs Margaret Lamunu John of the University of Juba for typing the manuscript and her patience as she had to cope with several corrections I made and which required her to sometimes retype the material.
I am confident that these colleagues and friends who have assisted me in various ways will find some satisfaction in the book, its shortcomings notwithstanding, for which I am alone responsible.

Abstract

The aim of this book is to investigate some aspects of the Dinka noun system. The book consists of five chapters and a conclusion. Chapter One surveys the general backgrounds of the Dinka people which include the social and historical backgrounds, the Dinka people and their locations, Dinka within the Nilotic languages and dialects of the Dinka language.

Chapter Two is a review of the literature on the Dinka language. Chapter Three is on Dinka phonology whose subsections include the tone in Dinka, the Dinka vowel system and the syllable.

Chapter Four deals with compounding, word-formation and cattle name prefixes. The main strategies for that are based on joining nouns with nouns, nouns with adjectives, nouns with verbs, singular nouns with possessive morphemes, plural nouns with plural possessive morphemes and demonstrative morphemes which are joined with nouns they point at or they describe. Chapter Five is a reduplication which is a repetition of all or some parts of a stem. It mostly forms abstract nouns.

However, the investigations reveal that Dinka nominal system involves so many complicated and intricate rules. Therefore, this review recommends a detailed study of all the Dinka dialects in order to be able to draw out Dinka language morphological rules.

Contents

Dedication	i
Acknowledgements	ii
Preface	iii
Abstract	iv

Chapter One

Introduction

1.0	Historical background to the Dinka	1
1.1	Early pre-history of the Dinka	1
1.2	The term Dinka and its implications	2
1.3	The Dinka people and their geographical distribution	3
1.4	Dinka within the Nilotic languages	4
1.5	The dialects of the Dinka	5

Chapter Two

Review of the literature on Dinka language   7

Chapter Three

3.0	On Dinka phonology	12
3.1	Tone in Dinka	12
3.2	The Dinka vowel system	14
3.3	The syllable in Dinka	16

Chapter Four

4.0 Dinka compounding, word formation and cattle name prefixes ... 17

4.1 **Compounding** ... 17
4.1.1 Noun-plus-noun compounds ... 20
4.1.2 Noun-plus-adjective compounds ... 21
4.1.3 Compounds formed by combining nouns with verbs ... 22

4.2 **Word Formation** ... 24

4.2.1 Possessive morphemes ... 25
(i) Singular nouns joined with possessive morphemes
(ii) Singular nouns joined with plural possessive morphemes
(iii) Plural nouns joined with plural possessive morphemes
4.2.2 **Demonstrative morphemes** ... 27
4.2.2.1 Demonstrative morphemes "e" (this) ... 27
4.2.2.2 Demonstrative morphemes "tui" (that) ... 29
4.2.2.3 Demonstrative morphemes "ke" (these) ... 30
    (i) "ke" as a suffix of a plural noun
    (ii) "ke" as a prefix as well as a suffix
4.2.2.4 Demonstrative morphemes "kui" (those) ... 31
4.3 **Cattle name prefixes** ... 33
4.3.1 Cattle name prefix "a" ... 33
4.3.2 Cattle name prefix "na" ... 34
4.3.3 Cattle name prefix "ma" ... 35
... 36

Chapter One

Introduction

1.0 Historical background to the Dinka

1.1 Early prehistory of the Dinka

The Dinka people call themselves "Jieeng" but the name by which they are best known is Dinka which also stands for their language. There is no recorded history as to when and from where the Dinka people came to their present home, but a few traces have been made by different historians.

Frank and Snowden (1970) states that the earlier Kushites conquered Egypt in 730 B.C and founded the twenty-fifth dynasty. Similarly, the people of Meroe (542 BCE – 339, 350 CE), used their military skills to further their territorial expansion and for many years occupied an area that expanded southward for Nuba in the north to what is now Sennar and Kosti. These historical facts testify the probable presence of African elements among the populations of Napata and Meroe. In this regard, Diodorus (first century BCE), tells us that "the majority of Ethiopians who dwelt along the Nile were black Africans; black skinned; flat noses and wholly haired". Likewise, Arkell (1949), states that the remains excavated from earlier site in Khartoum were submitted for examination and were found with central incisor teeth removed, which is a common practice among many African peoples in general and among the Dinka people in particular. This feature was again traced by Sir Henry welcome's (1912) excavation at Jebel Moya, a place situated less than 200 miles south of Khartoum and just over 20 miles west of Sennar. According to Arkell, the excavation in Khartoum mentioned earlier revealed that:

> The early inhabitants were living on low sand-bank at the edge of the Blue Nile; they resembled the present day Nilotic peoples such as the Dinka of Bor District who camp on the edge of the Nile in situations where they are liable to be flooded at higher river, and largely live by spearing fish and harpooning hippopotamus.

However, the probable presence of African elements in the Pharaonic civilization is also evident in Shinnie (1967), based on thorough study of three skulls of Meroitic origin excavated in the tomb of King Amanitenmemide (45-47 CE). Two of these skulls were found to be persons of black race.

From all the above assertions, it can be deduced that the Nilotic people were among the black Africans who were known to be the Ancient Egyptians, Greek and Romans. They lived in the kingdoms of Kush and Meroe. They might have moved southward to Khartoum, Sennar, Kosti and further to where they live today. It is thus, undoubtedly acceptable that Dinka were included in the migration.

1.2 The name "Dinka" and its connotations

The word "Dinka" stands the name used by the people who are known by outsiders Dinka. The Dinka call themselves Jieeng or Jiëëŋ. "Dinka" is a recent coinage which dates back to the period during which the Dinka people first came into contact with Arab inhabitants probably between 15th – 16th centuries CE as stated by Hasan (1973).

There is no agreement on origin of the word "Dinka" which continues to be a subject of debate even among the very people for which the name is applied. One of the popular surmises among the Dinka speakers is that the name owes its origin to a corruption of a man called Deng Kak. In the 19th century was a historical Deng Kak who was a chief of Abiliang people living in the area that became Renk district whose headquarters was- and continued to be- Renk town in northern Upper Nile region, not far from the border with Sudan.

Deng Kak was a powerful chief who maintained a good relationship with his neighbours to the north of his area. Arab traders had to get permission from him when they wanted to enter the Dinka territory on their trading missions. These traders used to refer to the Abiliang people- who are Dinka speakers - as the people of Deng Kak. This was in the course of time slightly changed and the Arabs gradually began to use the term (Deŋka) (Denka), singular/ *dengkawi/deŋkka:wi*). These changes ultimately gave rise to "Dinka" as the name and language of the people who call themselves Jieeng.

1.3 The Dinka people and their territorial distribution

The Dinka are tall, slender and fine featured Nilotic people in the present day Republic of South Sudan. Deng, F. M. (1973), asserts that the Dinka are among the tallest and blackest people in the world. They are a congeries (collection, mass) of independent sections spread over a vast area stretching over the 6^0 of latitude 12^0 to 6^0N from Renk in the north to Bor in the south with a wide extension to the west occupying much of Greater Bahr el Ghazal and Lakes State, and even crossing the

Bahr el Arab-known to South Sudanese as Kiir-into South Kordofan which is home to the Ngok Dinka.

The Dinka people are related to the Nuer. A legend relating the common ancestry mentioned by Butt (1952), states that; "Dengdit" (the legendary forebear of Dinka and Nuer) married a woman called "Alyet" in Dinka language and "Lit" in that of Nuer. Alyet or Lit gave birth to Akol who married Garang from whom descended the brothers Deng and Nuer being the ancestors of the present Dinka and Nuer. Such, then are the assertions of interrelationship of the two nationalities, and according to these hypotheses, there is a genetic relationship between the Dinka and Nuer.

Geographically, the Dinka are divided into sections as follows:

(a) The **Northern Dinka:** mainly situated in Upper Nile, extending south to Bahr el Zeraf, Lake No and Bahr el Ghazal. The main sections inhabiting this area are known as the Padang Dinka.

(b) **The Eastern Dinka:** situated on the right bank of the Nile from southeast of Ayod to Bor. The inhabitants are known as Dinka Bor.

(c) **The Central Dinka:** this group inhabits the area on the left bank of the Nile extending westwards to Tonj. This includes the Aliap, the Ciec, the Agaar and the Gok Dinka.

(d) **The Western Dinka:** situated west of Nuer and about the Jur River area from Tonj in the south and Kiir River in the north and west of Aweil. This area is inhabited by the Rek and Malual Dinka.

Administratively, the Dinka are included in six states of South Sudan. They are large in number and widespread in settlement. They are also found in Jonglei, Unity, Lakes, Warrap, Northern Bahr el Ghazal and Upper Nile states. Abyei is administered from Warrap in the region of Greater Bahr el Ghazal.

1.4 Dinka within the Nilotic languages

According to Greenberg's classification of African languages (1963), and in the subdivision of Nilotic languages, Dinka is a member of the western Nilotic family of languages. Its relatives are: Nuer, Collo (also known as Shilluk), Anywaa (previously known as Anyuak by outsiders), Burun, Acholi and Jur.

Beside its relationship to the above languages, Dinka has the following characteristics: first, the majority of its words are monosyllabic and the commonest syllable of these being CVC [consonant vowel consonant]; second, Dinka is a tone language; third, it has no gender distinction.

However, the extent of the western Nilotic languages as a whole is essentially the environs of the White Nile River and its tributaries from Renk in the far north to Kyogo in the south ($12°N$, latitude to $2°$ N latitude) and just to the northeast of Lake Victoria. According to B. Ogot, (1967) the Luo language groups, that is to say, the Southern Luo located in the south of environs of the eastern and western Nilotic languages, arrived in their present location five centuries ago in the first series of migrations from the north. According to B. Ogot, these migrations were part of a large dispersion of the Nilotic peoples over many centuries, from which groups split off and settled along the way. As the migrating groups diverged from each other, dialect differences that gave birth to different languages developed and the group came

6 SOME ASPECTS OF DINKA NOUN SYSTEM

into contacts with the speakers of alien languages that influenced their own.

1.5 The dialects of the Dinka language

As shown in the geographical division above Dinka has four major dialects and these include: the Eastern dialect which is Bor – based, the Northern Dialect which is known as Padang, which is Dongjol based, the Southern Dialect which is Agaar based and the Western dialect which is Rek – based. However there are minor variations within each major group. The differences that exist among the major groups, although greater than those within each major group, do not challenge the unity of an analysis that covers the whole Dinka language. The following is a list of the major dialects and where they are spoken and their closely related sub-dialects:

(a) **Bor Dialect** – is spoken by Bor Gok (Gɔ̈k) who call themselves Bor and around Bor Town on the right bank of the Nile. It is also spoken by Bor-Athooc (Athɔ̈ɔ̈c) who are known by their neighbours as Athoc (Athɔ̈c). Its closely related sub-dialects are: Twi, spoken by Twi people, Nyarweng–by Nyarweng people and Hol (Ɣɔ̈l) – spoken by Hol people. Twi (Twï), Nyarweng and Hol of Duk County are located at the far north of Bor.

(b) **Agaar Dialect** – spoken by the Agaar, southeast of Tonj, north of Rumbek. It is closely related to sub-dialects, Aliap, southeast of Agaar,Ciec (Ciëc) or Cic (Cïc) as they are sometimes known. These people live around Yirol and are neighbours of Agaar, Rek and Gok (Gɔ̈k). (The Gok people of Lakes State should not be confused with the Gok of Bor in Jonglei State.)

(c) **Rek Dialect** – spoken by the Rek people who live in Bahr el Ghazal. It is closely related to Luac (Luäc), east of Rek, Twic (Twïc) – north of Rek, Pallient – branch of Rek, Malual – between Kiir river in the north and the River Lol in the south.

(c) **Padang Dialect** – spoken by Padang, Abiliang and Dongjol on the right bank of the Nile opposite to Kodok area.

The Dinka language is also spoken as a second language by the tribes who are neighbours of the Dinka, particularly the Jur of Bahr el Ghazal who are neighbours of the Dinka, in Aweil and around Wau town, extending eastwards to Mbili. The Bongo people who are also neighbours of Dinka and who live together within Tonj town speak Dinka as a second or a third language. The Eastern Dialect which is Bor. The main speakers of this dialect are the Gok (Gɔ̈k) and Athooc (Athɔ̈ɔ̈c) people who inhabit southern and central parts of the former Bor district. Due to the influence of Malek, not far from Gok area, where an elementary school was opened at the beginning of the last century, the Bor dialect became the medium of instruction in what were known as bush schools in the entire Bor district. The early Church literature was written in that dialect which for years was also used in Yirol and Rumbek districts of the former Bahr el Ghazal province.

Chapter Two

Review of the literature on Dinka language

The existing literature on Dinka falls into two related areas:

Dinka orthography and Dinka language description including lexicography. In this chapter, I will try to give a brief and tentative review of literature in both areas hinted above.

The Christian missionaries are the pioneers in studying the vernacular languages of South Sudan. Their aim was to describe the grammar of these languages, produce lexicons and develop orthographies for use in the translation of Bible.

Among the missionaries and linguists who worked on Dinka was a Verona (from Italy) priest, Father Nebel who worked with Dinka Rek in Kuajok area. In his *Dinka Grammar* (1948), Nebel briefly discussed the orthography and phonetics of Dinka, out of which he listed twenty-seven alphabets. Out of these, he identified 20 consonants, seven vowels, and four central vowels [ä, ë, ï, ö]. The second parts of this book deals with grammatical elements such as nouns, verbs, and adjectives.

Nebel's other significant work is his Dinka English and English- *Dinka Dictionary*, (1954). In his dictionary, he also attempted some grammatical analysis, thus differentiating between singular noun and plurals, on one hand, and nominal and genitive case on the other.

A longer English – Dinka dictionary was produced by R. Trudinger (1944), in which he also identified four tones for Dinka: high, medium, low and a tone higher than normal which he marked (±H).

Tucker, A.N. and Bryan, M.A., (1956) in *Non-Bantu Languages of Northeastern Africa*, classified the African languages and described the Nilotic languages under four headings: Dinka as a single unit with examples from dialects, Nuer-Western Nuer, Northern Luo-Shilluk and Southern Luo-Kenya Luo. In this book, they also listed four dialects of the Dinka which are Bor, Padang, Agaar and Rek.

Similarly, Tucker and Bryan (1966), (*Linguistic Analysis on Non-Bantu Languages of North-Eastern Africa*), again described the Nilotic languages under the same headings and noted the presence of "hard" and "breathy" (hollow) voice quality in Dinka. They went further to say that Dinka has a multiple phoneme system consisting of seven to nine vowels pronounced with "hard" voice. On the other hand, tone and stress, word shape, structural elements, number, gender, case and pronouns were also dealt with.

Welmers, W. (1973), *African Language Structures* quoted the work of Talmage Wilson of the Presbyterian Church who worked among Padang Dinka and said: "Wilson's encounter with the breathy vowels led me to an analysis of positing three vowel qualities in Dinka. These vowel qualities are: very long vowels with an extreme articulatory position, breathy vowels of intermediate length and somewhat more central and very short centralized vowels". It is worth mentioning that Wilson identified seven vowel positions which Welmers took over from him.

Tucker, A.N., (1978). *Dinka Orthography*, attempted to establish the rules for Dinka spelling and word division, in which all the four Dinka dialects are represented. He further stated that there shall be seven vowel letters in Dinka orthography: (i, e, ɛ, a, ɔ, o, u,), with capitals (I, E, Ɛ, A, Ɔ, O, U).

According to Tucker, these letters represent the vowels in their normal forms, breathy and centralized forms. Furthermore, Tucker in this book described diphthongs, length of vowels, consonants, imported words (spelling of English names) especially in Geography to vernacular textbooks and everyday writing. At the end, Tucker notes that "since the first appearance of the rules, a feeling has arisen among students and writers of Dinka that questions concerning voice quality, vowel length, differentiation and tone needed more attention."

Ayom, E.B.G., (1980). *Some Aspects of Phonology and Nominal Plural Formation*, discusses aspects of Dinka phonology such as tone, vowels, consonants and nominal plurals. He also considered Greenberg's (1963), and Tucker and Bryan's (1956), classifications of African languages. In these classifications, Dinka place within the Nilotic language has been shown.

Malou, J, (1988). *Dinka Vowel System*, the first part of his book deals with an outline of Dinka phonology. The second part handles the definition of breathiness and its role in the language. The third part investigates the role of vowel length and central vowels. According to Malou, the investigations show that breathiness in Dinka is distinctive and that there are seventy-eight distinct vowel sounds in Dinka. However, the linguists whose aim was to contribute to the area of linguistics in Western Nilotic Languages were Tucker and Bryan and Welmers. Tucker and Bryan (1948), recognize the complicated nature of Dinka vowel system. They pointed out the existence of seven vowel contrasts. Welmer's on the other hand, finds Wilson's tentative analysis of Dinka vowel system together with the morphological alternations operating it as remarkable.

To mention a point of concord, these groups of linguists agree that there is uncertainty about the phonemic boundaries of the language in question. But they disagree in that Tucker and Bryan assume eight articulatory vowel positions instead of Welmer's seven positions.

Consequently, the series of literary work done on Dinka narrated above led to the translation of text dictionaries and compilation of grammars. A *New Testament*- or

Lëk Jöt in Dinka- was translated into Dinka Bor dialect which first came out in 1939, followed by Padang and others being Agaar and Rek dialects. This work also served the evangelical purpose as well as the basis of educational development among the speakers of Dinka as a mother tongue. Teaching of vernaculars in both missionary and government schools began, followed by the Christian religion.

In evaluating this literature, one would say that nothing greater has been done in Dinka since the major aim of the missionaries mentioned earlier and other scholars was to develop the Dinka orthography that could enable them to translate the scriptures and other occasional religious tracts in that language, and to learn the languages by themselves for easy communication among the Dinka people. Those pioneering linguists of the Dinka language neglected linguistic fields of studies such as phonology, morphology, syntax and semantics.

To date, the Summer Institute of Linguistics' office in Juba, in collaboration with the Government of South Sudan has produced primers at least in some selected languages spoken in South Sudan, among them the Bari, Dinka, Nuer, Zande, Moru, Lotuho and others.

For Dinka, a number of readers have been already produced. The development of Dinka orthography was the result of Rejaf Language Conference held in Rejaf in 1928. This conference recommended the adoption of the six South Sudan languages chosen for use in "Elementary Vernacular Schools." Dinka was one of these languages selected for use in education.

Chapter Three

3. Dinka Phonology

The outstanding phonological character in the Nilotic languages in general and in Dinka language in particular is the presence of both "hard" and "breathy" voice in the pronunciation of vowels, diphthongs and semi-vowels. Whereas in languages such as Moru, Zande and para- Nilotic languages, distinction in voice quality is bound up with distinction in vowel quality.

However, in the following paragraphs, I will try to give a few descriptions of the functions and the role played by tones, vowels and syllable in Dinka phonology.

3.1 Tone in Dinka

Ladefoged (1975), defines tone language as a language which has a pitch variation that affects the meaning of words. A more precise definition is provided by *Encyclopaedia Britannica* (1976), which describes tone as a unit used to distinguish one word from another that is otherwise identical in its sequence of consonant and vowels.

Following the above definitions, Dinka like most of African languages, is a tone language. Several linguists who have done some work on Dinka language have identified a number of tones. For instance, Tucker and Bryan (1948), and (1966), identify three tones, high (/), medium ( ) unmarked and low (\). Likewise, Duerken, J. and Agany. S (1982).

Introduction to Dinka Vowel System, identifies the same three tones. From the above identifications, it can be concluded that Dinka has three major tones which are high, medium and low, that are used in lexical contrast and word's distinction.

Tone in Dinka is used to contrast lexical items that differ solely by pitch as illustrated by the following examples:

(i) wàr - shoes (i) war shoes

    war - shoe   waar shoe

    wár change (command)   war change (command)

Tone serves also to signal morphological change of Dinka words whose roots are CVC in majority of cases. A typical example is shown in the generation of plurals from singular nouns as follows:

(ii) Pàny (walls) (ii) pëny walls

    Pány (wall)   päny wall

    dèŋ (rain)   deŋ rain

    déŋ (rains)   dëŋ rains

Moreover, it is employed to indicate a major modulatory contrast in morphology. For instance, it differentiates first person from second person singular. The high tone signals the second while the medium signals the first person singular. This tone contrast occurs on the auxiliary verbs as follows:

(iii) aba thöl bá lá bé (I will finish it so that you go home)

    Abà thöl ba lá béi (I finish it so that I go home)

Aside from all these, tones in Dinka have purely syntactic functions, that is to say, tone plays a very significant role in differentiating negation from the auxiliary "acï" (is, has ...and so on.)

(iv) yén ací lá   he is not going
     yén acì là   he has gone

It also differentiates active voice from passive voice, thus:

ɣén acì Deŋ muɔ̈ɔ̈th   I have greeted Deŋ

(ɣén ací Deŋ muɔ̈ɔ̈th)   I have been greeted by Deŋ

acì _____ with low tone expresses the active voice.

ací _____ with high tone indicates the passive voice.

3.2 The Dinka Vowel System

On the Dinka vowel system, Tucker and Bryan (1966) and Duerksen and Agany (1982), state that: "Dinka has eight contrastive vowel positions. Each of these eight vowels can be either short or long. The short vowels are marked by using the symbol (v) while the long ones are marked by two symbols (vv)"

Below is a diagram showing the eight vowel positions

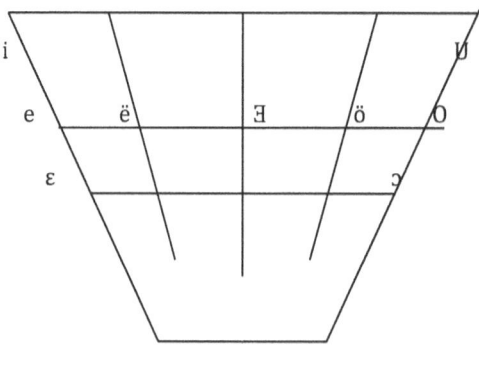

Ä

a

It is worth mentioning that the peripheral vowels may have both "breathy" and "hard" voices while the central vowels (ë, ə, ä, ö), have only breathy voice.

The presence of two voices in the pronunciation of vowels in Dinka made Tucker and Bryan again classify them into groups, the breathy is marked by two dots on the vowel (ë) and non-breathy left unmarked.

Catford, (1977) describes breathy vowels as a set of qualifiers determining a mode of glottal vibration different from normal, which is called modal voice. Stewart, (1971) describes non-breathy vowels as those frequently articulated with greater degree of muscular tension than the breathy vowels.

From the articulatory point of view, a breathy is produced by opening the vocal folds slightly, increasing the flow of air from the lungs and expanding the pharynx. Whereas non-breathy is produced with the body of the tongue domes upward, the larynx at the normal position and the vocal folds lying side by side, as stated by Laver (1980).

3.3 The Syllable

Described in terms of the elements distributed in it and features that characterize it, the syllable in Dinka is a unit of tone placement. Every syllable carries one and only one tone containing one and only one highest point of sonority is called the nucleus of the syllable as stated by MohrLang, (1972).

In Dinka, there are three syllable types, V, CV and CVC as exemplified below:

V-ë: yes
CV-ca: milk
CVC-mac: fire

The V syllable type has neither onset nor coda syllable margin. The vowel functioning as the syllable nucleus in V syllable is realized as shorter. The CV syllable type contains the majority of consonantal sounds functioning as onset margin and a good number of vowels functioning as nucleus. Thus, the following examples show the vowels that occur as nuclei in CV syllables.

/i/ yï - you (object)
/e/ ke – with
/u/ ku – and

The CVC syllable contains, on the other hand any of the consonantal sounds functioning as the onset margin and of the vowels as nucleus.

Chapter Four

4.0 Dinka Compounding, word formation and cattle name prefixes

In Dinka, words are generally joined together only when their juxtapositions indicate that a new concept or idea is formed with a more extensive meaning of the same words has taken separately.

Basically, this section will discuss compounding, word formation and cattle name prefixes. Compounds are formed by combining a noun with another noun, noun with adjective and a noun plus verb. On the other hand, word formation includes noun plus personal possessive morphemes, noun plus demonstrative morphemes, cattle name prefixes plus adjectival colours.

4.1 Compounding

The idea of compounding made different linguists to present their view points. Thus, Sloat, Taylor and Hoard (1978) define compounding as a combination of two or more roots without or with accompanying affixes. However, in compounding, new words may be formed by stringing together other words to create compounds. In English for example, compound nouns can be formed by combining noun with noun, noun with adjective, noun with verb, and so forth. These combinations can be illustrated below:

Noun + Noun – poorhouse
Noun + Adjective – headstrong
Verb + Noun – pick pocket

However, in compounding, the meaning of each compound word includes to some extent the meanings of the individual parts. But there are other compounds that do not seem to relate to the meanings of the individual parts.

On the other hands, it can be vindicated that two word compounds are the commonest in most languages in the world. Nevertheless, it would be difficult to state an upper limit in compounding as these English examples show: three-time-lesser, segment-in-arms, father-in-law, and so on. Although the examples given above are English examples; this does not mean that English alone displays compounding (but other languages in the world do). For example:

In Twi (one of the languages of Ghana): ɔba (child), ɔhene (chief) ɔheneba (prince)

In Thai: MEEU (cat), fäw (watch), baan (house), MEEU fäw baan (cat watch house)

In Papago: hazichu (thing), doakam (living creature), hazichudaokam (animal life)

In Nuer: duel (house), gɔrä (writing), duelgɔrä (school)

In Shilluk: ɔt (house), gwɛt (writing). ɔtgwɛt (school)

In French: cure (picking), dent (tooth), cure dent (tooth picking)

In Spanish: toca (to put), discos (record), tocadiscos (record player)

In Dinka: pan (house), akïm (doctor), panakïm (hospital)

Furthermore, Fromkin and Rodmon (1980) describe compounding as a common and frequent process for enlarging the vocabulary of all languages. It is also important to note that, in compounding the meaning of compounds must be learned as if they are individual words.

One of the most important morphophonemic processes involved in compounding and word formation in Dinka pertains to consonantal changes in certain morphological environment. Here singular nouns ending with voiceless consonants change their final consonants to nasals. This change to nasals takes place when a noun which ends with a voiceless consonant is followed and joined with another noun or adjective. The follow are examples:

p > m: líép (tongue) = rááń (person), liem e raan (person's tongue)

t > n: ɤɔt (house, hut) = töc (lying down) = yɔnetöc (sleepingroom)

c > ny: moc (man) dït (big) = monydït (an old man)

k > y: tik (woman), thi (small) = tiŋthi (younger wife) tiŋthi

th > nh: Nhialic (God)dit(big) = Nhialinydit (Almighty)

Plural nouns ending with voiceless final consonants, followed, joined with other plural nouns or adjectives will not change their voiceless final consonants to nasal as do the singular above. For instance,

p > m: tíɔp (soil) cöl (black), tíɔm cöl (black soil) tiɔp (tiɔm) col **p>p:** tiɔp (soil col

t > t: ɣööt (houses) nhiim (heads) = ɣöötnhïïm (tops of houses)

c > c: mɛ́c (fire), atóóc (fishermen) = mɛ́c atóóc (fishermen fires)

k > k: jak (spirits) rac (bad) = jakrac (devils or satans)

th > th: ròth (hippos) cúái (fat) = ròth cúái (fat hippos)

The consonantal change explained above, always prevails in the final consonant of the first element of a compound or formed morphemes. It usually occurs wherever a possession is involved or when something belongs to something.

4.1.1 Noun-plus-Noun Compounds

These compounds are formed by one noun with another. Assimilation of voiceless final consonants in the first elements of compounds and shortening of long vowel may be involved in some cases as can be seen below:

Noun	+Noun	Compound	Gloss
Gloss			
aríik (lizard) +	kòòr (lion)	Aríŋ kòòr	(ab silik)
tík (woman) +	báái (home)	tíŋbáái	(housewife)
tím (tree) +	nhóm (head)	tímnhóm	(tree's top)
méth (child) +	thúkúl (school)	ménhthúkúl	(pupil)
pán (home,house)+	akím (doctor)	pánakím	(hospital)
pán (home, house) +	nhíál (sky)	pánnhíál	(heaven)

'ɔt (house) +   Nhíálic (God)   ɣɔ'nnhíálic   (church)
ɣ'ɔt (house) +   gàär(writing)   ɣɔ'ngààr   (school)
búk (book) +   Nhíálic (God) búŋnhíálic   (Bible)
kuér (road) +   thók (mouth) kuérthók   (doorway)

Observation

From the examples on the formation of compound words through joining noun with noun, the following can be observed:

In the first noun set, eight examples carry high tones while the remaining two examples bear low tones for instance,

ɣɔ't and ɣɔ't differently used.

In the second noun set or the second element of a compound, eight examples also possess high tones. For example, kòòr and gààr. See above for high tones. Moreover, in the compound set, the two examples in the second noun set which exhibit low tones just mentioned above and which are second elements of compounds, still maintain their low tones. The remaining examples bear high tones as the investigator can see above. Furthermore, the following singular nouns have changed their final consonants to nasals:

k > ŋ   arík > aríŋkòòr
k > ŋ   tík > tíŋbáái
k > ŋ   búk > búŋ Nhíálic
th > nh   méth > ménhthúkúl
t > n   ɣɔ't   > ɣɔ'nhíálic
t > n   ɣɔ't   > ɣɔ'ngààr

In this compound formation category, high tones are predominant.

4.1.2 Noun + adjective compounds

These compounds are formed by joining noun with adjective. Adjectives combined with these nouns follow the nouns to which they are joined as second elements of compounds.

Like the previous examples in 4.1.1, singular nouns which are the first elements of compound joined with adjectives to form compounds, in the following examples may change their final consonants to nasals according to the Dinka rule.

Noun	Adjective	Compound	Gloss
tík (woman) dít(big)		tíŋdít	elder wife
tík (woman)	lúɔ'm (illegal)	tíŋlúɔ'm	ocncubine
bèny (chief)	dít(big)	bɛnydít (Lord, refers to God)	
pál (knife)	dít(big)	páldít	(cutlass)
ráán (person)	dít(big)	rándit	(an elder)
jɔ'k (Spirit)	rác (bad)	jɔ'ŋrác	(devil, Satan)

Commenting on the above examples, it can be stated that, in the noun category, almost all the examples carry high tones with the exception of only one example which carries a low tone, for example, bëny.

In the adjectival group, the high tones are regular whereas the compound set behaves like the noun category, where only bɛny continues to maintain its low tone.

/k/ in these examples, changes to /ŋ/.

Thus, **k > tik > tiŋdït**
k > tik > tiɛŋluɔm
k > jɔk > jɔŋrac

4.1.3 Compounds Formed by Combining Nouns with Verbs

Although it is of rare occurrence in Dinka language, a noun can be joined with a verb to form a compound. In the process of forming compounds by joining nouns with verbs, two significant units can be identified. First, (e) which always comes before a verb, is a present simple tense marker. Secondly, "ke" which occurs as a suffix of a verb is a plural marker. Thus, in the following examples, singular nouns are joined with verbs:

Noun   Adjective   Compound Gloss   Noun Adjective Compound   Gloss

raan (person)   piööc   raanpiööc (teacher)   teacher
kɔc (people)   piööcke (training)   kɔcpiööcke   disciples

"ke" refers to plural.

Móc (man)   thíék (marrying)   Mónythíék   (Bridegroom)   moc   (man) thiëk (marrying)   monythiëk   bridgeroom

The following are nouns plus verbs with the present simple tense marker (e). They are written separately in Dinka but have single referents in English. Thus,

ráán(person)   e lím (he begs) rán e lím (beggar)   raan (person)   e lim (he begs)   ran e lim   beggar

ráán(person)   e thál (he cooks), ráán e thál (cook) raan (person   e thal (he cooks)   raan e thal   cook

ɣɔ't (house, hut)   e thál (hut used for cooking)   ɣöt (house, hut)   e thal ( )   yön e thal   kitchen

ɣɔ'nethál (kitchen)

Kɔ'c (people) e thath (they forge)kɔ'c e thath (black smiths) kɔc (people) e thäth (they forge metal) kɔc e thäth   blacksmiths

Kɔ'c (people) e púr (they cultivate)kɔ'c e pur (cultivators) kɔc (people)   e pur
(they cultivate)   kɔc e pur   cultivators

Ròr (men)   e yík (they build)   ròreyík (builders) röör (men)   e yïk
(they build)   rööreyïk   builders

Tùŋ (horn) e cám (used for eating)   tùŋecám(spoon) tuŋ (horn)   e cäm
(used for eating)   tuŋecäm   spoon

From the above examples on noun plus verb compounds, it is realized that, high tones in the noun set are predominant with only three examples exhibiting low tones e.g. ɣòt, ròr and tùŋ.

In the verbal set, all the verbs carry high tones while in the compound set, the compounds possess predominant high tones. Only two examples are first elements of compounds maintain their low tones, for example, röör and tuŋ. Their partners which are the second elements of compounds possess high tones, for example, yïk and cäm. See above.

"ke" and "e" carry mid tones.

Moreover, a noun with a long vowel has shortened its long vowel the compound for example, ráán > rán e lím, ran e thál and raanpiööc. Also, the following singular nouns have changed their voiceless final consonants to nasals:

c > ny móc > monythiëk

t > n ɣöt > ɣön e thal

For this section, one can conclude that high tones are as can be observed in 4.11, 4.1.2 and 4.1.3 examples. Nouns and adjectives which are second components of compounds that have long vowels did not change and do not shorten their long vowels. For example, tiŋbáái in 4.1.1 and ɣɔ'ngààr ɣönegäär in 4.1.2 but singular nouns which are always the first elements of compounds do shorten their long vowels, thus: ráán > rándit randït in 4.1.2.

4.2 Word Formation

In Dinka language, personal possessive morphemes are not defined in isolation of nouns but they are joined together. For instance dom (garden), die dïe (my), domdie domdï (my garden). Similarly, demonstrative morphemes do not do without being joined to the nouns they point at, thus, wut (camp) e (this), wunë (this camp) ráán(person) túi (that) rántúi (that person) and so on for other demonstrative morphemes.

Also, cattle name prefixes are not meaningful units in Dinka language unless they are joined with adjectival colours to give proper names for cattle members. Thus: á refers to female cattle prefix, yén (fawn colour) ayén (tan cow). "Ná" refers to calf prefix, yäär (white colour) náyár (white heifer). "Má" refers to male cattle prefix jök (white and black), majök white and black male).

Moreover, verbs form abstract nouns when they are reduplicated, for example, *muk* (keep imperative) *mukmuk* (keeping)

According to the above morphological rule, the following section is a joining of morphemes that do not semantically mean compounds but they are joined to give other meanings as the language detects. These include: noun plus possessive morphemes, noun plus demonstrative morphemes, cattle name prefixes plus adjectival colours and reduplication.

4.2.1 Possessive morphemes

In Dinka, personal possessive morphemes are joined to the nouns they follow. In this group, singular nouns are joined with singular possessive morphemes and plural possessive morphemes. Also, plural nouns are joined with plural possessive morphemes.

(i) Singular nouns joined with the singular possessive morphemes:

Die (my), du (your), de (his, her, its)

Noun	Possessive morphemes	Gloss
rïŋ (meat)	rïŋdie	my meat
weŋ (cow)	weŋdu	your cow
pɛɛm (chest)	pɛmde	his chest

(ii) Singular nouns joined with plural possessive morphemes:

da (our), dun (your plural), den (their)

Noun	Plural Possessive Morphemes	Gloss Noun
laŋ (nim tree)	laŋda	our need tree
thɔn (bull)	thɔndun	your bull
töny (pot)	tönyden	their pot

(iii) Plural nouns joined with plural possessive morphemes:

kuɔ (our), kun (your), ken (their)

Noun	Pl. Possessive Morphemes	Gloss
luëk (byres)	luëkkuɔ	our byres
kuɛɛr (footpaths)	kuɛrkuɔn	your footpaths
kuar (grandfathers)	kuarken	their grandfathers

Observation

From the above examples on the possessive morphemes joined with singular and plural nouns, it can be realized that: in the category (i) die and de possessive morphemes carry high tones while du possesses a low tone. These possessive morphemes maintain their tones even when they are joined to nouns. Also, in this category, all the nouns in the noun set bear high tones of which one example has a long vowel which became shortened after it has been joined with possessive morpheme, for example, pɛɛm > pɛ́mdé.

In category (ii), two examples exhibit high tones thus, láŋ and thɔ'n while the remaining one carried a low tone, for example, tòny. The plural possessive morphemes in these categories possess high tones, thus, dá, dún and dén.

In category (iii) both plural nouns and plural possessive morphemes have regular high tones as can be seen above. In a similar manner, the above rule can be used for the following expressions:

Nyuɔ̈cë në camdie   (sit to the left of my side)

Laarë në ciindu   (take it with your hand)

Cɔk wec në cökke   (let him kick it with his feet)

These examples show only singular possession as well as intimacy since cam, ciin, and cook are all parts of the body.

4.2.2 Demonstrative Morphemes

Dinka like many African languages and other languages in the world, has four demonstrative morphemes, thus, "e" (this), "tui" (that), "ke" (these), and "kui" (those). These demonstrative morphemes are always joined with the nouns they point at or they describe. Thus, in this subsection, singular nouns are joined with the singular demonstrative morphemes whereas the plural nouns are joined with the plural demonstrative morphemes.

Singular nouns ending with voiceless final consonants such as /p/, /t/, /c/, /k/, and /th/) changed their consonants to nasal /m/, /n/, /ny/, /ŋ/, and /nh/) according to the rule provided above. Plural nouns ending with these voiceless final consonants will not change to nasals, as this rule is also provided above.

4.2.2.1 Demonstrative Morpheme "e" (this)

"e" is a demonstrative morpheme in Dinka which means (this) in English. It usually comes at the end of a noun which it describes and to which it is joined as a suffix, however, the following examples show how the demonstrative morphemes can be joined with nouns: -

Noun	Demonstrative Morpheme	Gloss
yith (well)	yinnhë	this well
wëër (cow-dung)	wére	(this cow-dung)
waar (shoe)	warë	(this shoe)
dhɔk (boy)	dhɔŋë	(this boy)
thööc (chair)	thönyë	(this chair)
kuur (stone)	kurë	(this stone)

Analyzing on this group of nouns joined with the demonstrative morpheme "e", one can say that joining a noun with a demonstrative morpheme does not change the meanings of the original individual words or the joined morphemes. For instance, yith > yinhë (this well). Both **yith** and **e** maintain their meanings. Only "**th**" has changed to "**nh**" according to the rule of consonant nasal change illustrated above.

In this noun set of these examples, all the nouns carry high tones. The demonstrative morpheme (e) joined with noun continues to maintain its mid tone. On the other hand, singular nouns have changed their final consonants to nasals e.g.

th > nh → yith > yinhë (this well)
k > ŋ → dhök > dhöŋë (this boy)
c > ny → thööc > thönyë (this chair)

Moreover, a singular noun with a long vowel has shortened its long vowel thus; kuur > kurë.

4.2.2.2 Demonstrative morpheme tui (that)

"Tui" is a demonstrative morpheme in Dinka which represents "that". It always follows the singular noun which it described and to which it is joined. Thus, the following examples reveal how the demonstrative morpheme "tui" is joined to a number of singular nouns:

Noun	Demonstrative Morpheme	Gloss
tím (tree)	tímtúi	(that tree)
léŋ (drum)	léŋtúi	(that drum)
déél (tuft grass)	déltúi	(that tuft grass)
ráán (person)	rántúi	(that person)
túɔ'ŋ (egg)	tuɔŋtui	(that egg)
cɔɔe (blind man)	cɔɔrtui	(that blind man)
cól (a piece of charcoal)	cóltúi	(that piece of charcoal)
púúr (hoe)	púrtúi	(that hoe)

One of the significant things that can be realized in the above examples is that a number of singular nouns possessing long vowels have shortened their long vowels after they are joined with the demonstrative morpheme "tui". For example:
-

dɛ́ɛ́l > dɛ́ltúi

rááń > rántúi

cɔɔr > cɔrtui

púúr > púrtúi

Also, it can be seen above that all the nouns in the noun set of "tui" examples carry high tones. Demonstrative "tui" which is joined with the noun as seen in the demonstrative morpheme set, maintains its high tone also. Thus, high tones are regular all over this category.

4.2.2.3 Demonstrative Morpheme "ke"

In describing the plural nouns in Dinka, the demonstrative morpheme (ke) is used, in most cases it occurs as a suffix of a plural noun than a prefix. Sometimes it occurs as prefix and as a suffix of a plural noun it describes at the same time. For instance, "ke" – mïthke > (these children)

It is to be noted that "ke" only occurs as a prefix when it is also occurring as a suffix, i.e. you can not say ke pɛi or ke lài but you can say kepëikë (these months) and keläikë (these animals).

(i)   "**Ke**" as a suffix of the plural noun.

In these examples, "ke" will occur once as a suffix to plural nouns it may describe.

| **Noun** | **Plural Demonstrative Morpheme** | **Gloss** |

nyïïr (girls)	nyïïrkë	these girls
bëi (homesteads)	bëikë	these homesteads
dël (skins)	dëëlkë	these skins
bäny (chiefs)	bänykë	these chiefs
tɔɔŋ (spears)	tɔɔŋkë	these spears
cök (feet)	cökkë	these feet
tuŋ (horns)	tuŋkë	these horns

From the above category, the following features can be identified: in the plural noun set, five examples carry high tones, for example, nyïïr, bëi. bäny, tɔɔŋ and tuŋ. While the other two examples which also possess breathiness carry low tones e.g. dèl, and còk. These two examples still maintain their low tones after they are even joined with demonstrative morpheme "ke" as in dëlkë, cökke.

"ke: as a prefix as well as a suffix.

The demonstrative morpheme "ke" sometimes occurs as a prefix and as a suffix of a plural noun it describes at the same time as follows:

Plural	Plural Demonstrative Morpheme	Gloss
dëŋ (rains)	kedëŋkë	these rains
läi (animals)	keläikë	these animals
köör (lions)	kekörkë	these lions
röör (men)	keröörkë	these men
kuëc (leopards)	kekuëckë	these leopards

One thing which is very clear in the above examples on joining plural nouns with demonstrative morpheme (ke) is that, all the plural nouns in the plural noun set carry low tones. Among these, two examples possess breathiness, for example, läi, and röör and one example carries centralization, for example, köör. "ke" occurs as a prefix and as a suffix as can be seen above with its constant mid tone.

4.2.2.4 Demonstrative Morpheme "kui" (those)

"Kui" is a plural demonstrative morpheme in Dinka which means "those". It is always joined with plural nouns which it follows as a suffix. Like in "ke" (these) examples above, plural nouns that are joined with "kui" do not change their final consonants to nasals as do the singular nouns in 4.2.2.1 and 4.2.2.2 above.

The following examples show how "kúi" is joined to plural nouns:

Plural Noun	Plural Demonstrative Morpheme	Gloss
nyïn (eyes)	nyïnkui	those eyes
rëc (fish plural)	reckui	those fish
mëc (fires)	mëckui	those fires
rak (fences)	rakkui	those fences

Plural Noun	Plural Demonstrative Morpheme	Gloss
tɔɔŋ (spears)	tɔɔŋkui	(those spears)
cöör (blind men)	cöörkui	(those blind men)
kur (stones)	kurkui	(those stones)

In the combination of plural nouns with the demonstrative morpheme "kúi" as illustrated above, it can be observed that: in the plural noun set, four examples exhibit high tones, for example, rëc, rak, tɔɔŋ, and kur. Three examples bear low tones for examples, nyïn, mëc and cöör. "kúi" carried a high tone. Both plural nouns and demonstrative "kúi" joined together under plural demonstrative morpheme; maintain their tones as can be seen above. To conclude this subsection on the demonstrative morphemes discussed above, one can reiterate that high tones show a sign of multiplicity among the given examples. Whereas low and mid tones have an insignificant occurrence. Breathiness and centralization of vowels also have a limited prevalence. Moreover, a change from final consonant to nasal is acknowledged among the singular nouns joined with singular demonstrative morphemes, a feature which is absent among the plural nouns joined with plural demonstrative morphemes. There are a few examples showing a shortening of a long vowel in the singular nouns joined with demonstrative morphemes.

4.3 Cattle Name Prefixes

In Dinka, cattle name prefixes such as a, na and ma are joined to adjectival colours to denote cattle names. Thus, "a" denotes a feminine cattle name, na denotes a calf and "ma" denotes masculine cattle name. Each of these will be discussed separately below:

4.3.1 Cattle Name Prefix "a"

As mentioned before, "a" refers to a feminine cattle name prefix. It is joined to an adjectival colour to indicate a female cattle name, for example, yén (grey colour), when we add "a" to yén it becomes áyén which means grey cow. Similar examples are provided below:

Adjectival Colour	Cattle Name Prefix	Gloss
luɛɛl (red)	aluɛɛl	red cow

kɔ̈l (red with white)   akɔ̈l   red with white cow

këër (black and white)   akëër   black and white cow

After joining prefix "a" with the above adjectival colours, the result is the cattle names which are mainly for females or cows. Thus, "a" prefix plays a role in naming the masculine cattle in Dinka.

In these examples also, adjectives in the adjectival set got two examples with low tones, for example, kɔ̈l and këër. The remaining one example carried high tone, for example, luɛɛl. The female cattle names discussed under cattle name prefix, all possess high tones.

4.3.2 Cattle Name Prefix "na"

"Na" is another cattle name prefix which occurs to different adjectival colors to denote a heifer in Dinka. For example, cóól which means (black colour) plus ná becomes nácóól which means a black heifer. Below, a number of adjectival colours have been assigned to ná prefix, joined together to indicate the heifer's name.

Adjectival Colour Cattle Name Prefix   Gloss

lith (silver-grey)   nalith   silver-grey heifer

jök (black and white)   najök   black and white heifer

yɔ̈r (white)   nayäär   white heifer

thiëëŋ (dark brown)   nathiëŋ   dark brown heifer

Like in a prefix examples, na - prefix is joined in the above examples with the adjectival colours to give the heifer's name as illustrated above. Na as an

34   SOME ASPECTS OF DINKA NOUN SYSTEM

individual morpheme carries a high tone. Also, in the adjectival set, two examples possess high tones while the remaining two bear low tones. See above.

The heifer's name set described under cattle name prefix above, caries high tones with the exception of one example shared by both high and low tones.

4.3.3   Cattle Name Prefix "ma"

Like the previous two "Ma" is a cattle name prefix that refers to male cattle. It is joined with different adjectival colours to denote a masculine cattle name as its partners do above. For example, cäär means black. Macäär means a black bull. Similar examples are provided below:

Adjectival Colour   Male Cattle Name Prefix Gloss

Adjectival Colour	Male Cattle Name Prefix	Gloss
bil (black and white spot)	mábil	black and white spot bull
këër (black and white)	makëër	black and white bull
yäär (white)	mayäär	white bull
löu (ash-grey)	malöu	ash-grey bull
bok (redish-grey)	mabok	reddish-grey bull
lual (red)	malual	red bull

As do a and na prefixes above, ma – prefix in these examples carries a high tone as an individual morpheme before it is joined to any adjectival colour. In the adjectival group, it can be observed that four examples possess high tones for example, bil, löu, bok, and lual. The other two examples possess low tones for instance, këër, yäär.

In the bull's name set described under male cattle name prefix above, both the adjectival and cattle name prefix joined together still maintain their previous mentioned high and low tones as can be seen above.

Chapter Five

Reduplication

Sloat, Taylor and Hoard (1978) describe reduplication as a repetition of all or some parts of a stem. In this connection, Elbert (1970) presented examples of reduplication in Hawaiin language to form the following morphemes:

holo (run)   holoholo (go for a walk)

lalu (leaf)   laulau (leaf food package)

polu (pleasant)   polupolu (pleasant or cool)

Like Hawaiin and other languages in the world, Dinka uses reduplication of words to form meaningful morphemes or abstract nouns. In most cases, this is done through reduplicating imperative or infinitive verbs in Dinka as shall be explained below: -

Verb	Verb reduplicated (Abstract noun)	Gloss
rír (to mix)	rírrír	confusion
lɛ́ŋ (to swing)	lɛ́ŋlɛ́ŋ	swinging
gòt (write-imperative)	gòtgòt	writing
kùm (cover-imperative)	kùmkùm	coverage

ríéth (to slip)   ríéth ríéth   slippery place
ŋùɛ́ŋ (to hesitate)   ŋùɛ́ŋ ŋùɛ́ŋ   hesitation

Observation

In the above examples on reduplication, observations reveal that the reduplicated verbs form meaningful morphemes which are termed as reduplicated morphemes or abstract nouns. Also, it is observed that in the verbal groups, three examples carry high tones, for example, rir, lɛŋ, and rieth. On the other hand, three examples from the same group carry low tones, thus, gɔ̈t, kum and ŋuëŋ.

Similarly, in the abstract noun set, three examples possess high tones whereas the other three bear low tones as respectively shown below:
High tones: rírrír, lɛ́ŋlɛ́ŋ and ɤíéth ɤíéth.
Low tones: gòt gòt, kùm kùm, and ŋuëŋ ŋuëŋ.

One example in the reduplicated morpheme set or abstract noun set does not relate to the meaning of the original verb after reduplication that is: rír (mix), rírrír (confusion).

To draw a conclusion this section, one can comment, in subsection 4.1.1 which is on compounding, high tones are remarkably predominant as shown by many examples provided.

However, a consonantal change to nasal occurred only among the singular nouns in 3.1.1 and 3.1.2 and 3.1.3 categories, it is absent among the plural nouns as the rule above prohibits it.

In 3.1.3, there is a group of nouns and verbs with e̱ present simple tense marker written separately but represents single referents in English. For instance: kɔc e̱ thal (cooks), kɔc e̱ thäth (blacksmiths) and so forth. Breathiness, centralization of vowel, shortening of long vowels, low tone and mid tones are present but not of frequent occurrence as is the high tones hinted above.

On 3.2 that are on word formations, it is to be recognized that possessive and demonstrative morphemes do not operate in isolation of nouns. Thus, singular nouns are always joined with singular possessive morphemes or singular demonstrative morphemes. Plural nouns, on the other hand, are joined with plural possessive morphemes. Other plural morphemes are also joined with singular nouns to indicate a single item possessed by many people or what belongs to many things.

Similarly, cattle name prefixes are not operating in the absence of adjectival colours but they are joined to them to give proper cattle names according to what each refers to.

Also, it is to be remarked that singular possessive morphemes, plural possessive joined with singular nouns and plural possessive joined with plural nouns carry high tones except one example which bears a low tone dù. Conversely, demonstrative morphemes, both singular and plural possess high tones with the exception of e, which exhibits a mid tone. Moreover, cattle name prefixes a, na and ma do the same done by singular and plural above. Reduplication behaves differently by repeating verbs to form abstract nouns.

Conclusion

I have tried in this book to examine and highlight various rules of nominal morphology of Dinka language, which is found to be based on both segmental and supra-segmented strategies. The introductory Chapter One includes notes on social and historical backgrounds of the Dinka with a particular focus on their early history. The scanty so far existing evidences, in the form of excavated material tend to place the Dinka among the African Nilotic people who lived in the kingdoms of Kush and Meroe, and who migrated southward through Khartoum, Sennar, Kosti and to their present habitat.

Further regional sub-migrations resulted as usual in their language being split into four recognized and actually intelligible dialects: Agaar, Padang, Rek and Bor (the present book is based on the latest dialect).

Chapter Two is the existing literature on Dinka which falls under two related areas: Dinka orthography and Dinka language description, including lexicography. Chapter Three is on Dinka phonology which discusses tones, vowel system and syllables. Chapter Four deal with compounding and word-formation which involves the forming of nouns with another, noun with adjective, noun with possessive morphemes and demonstrative morphemes with nouns.

Chapter Five is a reduplication of verbs to form abstract nouns. As can be seen above, Dinka nominal system involves so many complicated and intricate rules which can not be settled up in a research centered on one dialect such as the one in question. In the light of this fact, this book recommends a detailed study of all the Dinka dialects in order to be able to draw out Dinka language morphological rules.

References

1- Frank, Fr. and Snowden, M, (1970). *Blacks in Antiquities, Ethiopians in the Greco-Roman Experience*. The Belknap Press of Harvard University Press, Cambridge, Massachusetts, p. 114.

2- Napata, (751 – 542 BCE). This was the capital of Kush Kingdom. Its site is near the Fourth Cataract. Archaeologists tell us that the city's population was a mixture of Caucasians and black-skinned peoples.

3- Arkell, J.A. (1949). *Early Khartoum*. Oxford University Press, London. p.101.

4- Shinne, P.L., (1967). *Meroe Civilization of the Sudan*, Frederick, A. Praeger, New York: Washington, pp.154 – 156.

5- Hasan. Y.F. (1967). *The Arabs and the Sudan*, Edinburgh University Press, 22 George Square Edinburgh p.73.

6- Nebel, P.A. (1948). *Dinka Grammar*. Verona Mission Wau.

7- "The Aspect of Orthography" presented by Nebel in his *Dinka Grammar*, which distinguishes only vowels, central vowels and consonants is inadequate for scientific purpose.

8- Tucker, A.N. and Bryan, M.A, (1956). *Non-Bantu Languages of North Eastern Africa with the Supplement on the Non-Bantu Languages of South Africa*, by E.O. J. Westphal, Oxford University Press, London, pp.94 – 98.

9- Tucker, A.N. and Bryan, M.A, (1966). *Linguistics Analysis of Non-Bantu Languages of North Eastern Africa.* Oxford University Press, London, pp. 402–442.

10- Welmers, W., (1973). *African Language Structures.* University of California Press. Berkeley, Los Angeles, London, p. 28.

11- Greenberg, J.H., (1966). *The Language of Africa,* Mouton, the Hague, p. 85

12- Government report, (1928). *Rejaf Language Conference.* Oxford University Press, London, pp. 14 – 15 and Appendix II p. 46.

13- Ladetoged, P.N. (1975). *A Course in Phonetics.* Harcourt, Brace and Jovanovich, Chicago, p.225

14- Catford, J.C., (1977) *Fundamental Problems of Phonetics.* Indiana University Press, Bloomington. p.99

15- Stewart, J.M. 1971), "Niger-Congo Kwa" in *Current Trends in Linguistics:* the sub-*Saharan Africa*. Ed., by T. Sebeok and others. Mouton, The Hague, p. 198.

16- Laver, J. (1980). *The Phonetic Description of Voice Quality.* Oxford University Press. London, p. 132.

17- Robins, R.H., 1964. *General Linguistics, an Introductory Survey.* William Clowes and Sons Limited, London Beccles pp. 257 – 258.

18. Fromkin, V., Robert Rodman (1983). *An Introduction to language.* Holt, Rinehart, and Winston. New York, p. 117.

Appendix

The current Dinka orthography has fonts that indicate breathy vowels indicated by diacritics. For example, before the introduction of the system in the late 1970s readers could only use context to differentiate words such as "deŋ" or "riŋ" and their occurring in a text. Thanks to the system a writer can hardly make a mistake in regard to pronunciation and meanings. With the two words above as examples, the following words emerge:

Old form

The following are given as examples: deŋ (rain); deŋ (rains); deŋ (wreathe with pain), and riŋ (meat); riŋ (run) respectively. In the absence of the breathy symbol over /e/ or /i/ and in the absence of a context as a guide, the reader will be at a loss regarding pronunciation and meaning. In the new form as shown below, the symbol serves as a guide to meaning and pronunciation to some extent as will be seen below.

New Form

And with the introduction of the diareses (such as /ä/, /ë/, /ö/ and so on), we now have the following: deŋ (rain); dëŋ (rains); dëŋ (wreathe with pain). Although the last two have breathy /ë/ they differ in tone in that the first has high tone while the second has a low tone. As for "riŋ" we have the following: rïŋ (meat); riŋ (run). Despite the improvement resulting from the introduction of diacritics, problems in semantics and pronunciation remain. For example, without a tone sign alongside diacritic mark over a vowel to enhance understanding whether the tone is high, middle or low, identification of voice quality and meanings are incomplete. This is exactly the case in all the examples given in Dinka words, phrases or sentences given to illustrate some points. Because of that problem, all the examples in which words were marked with high or low tone but without diacritics are reproduced below for the benefit of the reader.

Dinka	English
War	shoes
päny	wall
pëëny	walls
deŋ	rain
dëŋ	rains

(iv) **Sentences used to indicate high or low tone**

Dink	English
Yeen acï lɔ	He has gone
Yeen acïe lɔ	He is not going
Ƴɛn acï Deŋ muɔ̈ɔ̈th	I have greeted Deng
Ƴɛn acïe Deŋ muɔ̈ɔ̈th	I have not greeted Deng

Word change resulting from compounding

p > m: lie**p** (tongue) = raan (person), lie**m** raan (a person's tongue)

t > n: ɣöt (house, hut) = tɔc (lying down),   ɣön e tɔc (a house for sleeping in)

c > ny: mo**c** (man) dït (big) = mo**ny**dït (an old man)

k > ŋ: ti**k** (woman) thi (small) = ti**ŋ**thi (junior wife)

th > nh: Nhiali**c** (God) dït (big) = Nhiali**ny**dït (Supreme God)

t > t: ɣöö**t** (houses) = ɣöö**t**nhïim (houses' tops)

c > c: më**c** (fires) = më**c**atooc (fishermen's fires)

k > k: ja**k** (spirits) rac (bad) = ja**k**rac (devils, satans)

4. 1. 1. Noun + noun

	compound	gloss
ariik (lizard + köör (lion)	arieŋköör	ab silik
tik (woman) + abaar (orphan)	tiɛŋabaar	widow
tim (tree) + nhom (top)	timnhom	tree's top
meth (child) + thukul (school)	mɛnhthukul	pupil
pan (home, house) + akïm (doctor)	panakïm	hospital
pan (home, house) + nhial (sky)	pannhial	heaven
ɣöt (house) + Nhialic (God)	ɣön Nhialic	church
ɣöt (house) + gäär (writing)	ɣön e gäär	school
buk (book) + Nhialic (God)	buŋ Nhialic	Bible
kueer (footpath) + thok (mouth)	kuerthok	exit

Changes of compounds affected by adding adjectives to nouns

Noun	Adjective	Compound	Gloss
tik (woman)	dït (big)	tiŋdït	elder wife
tik (woman)	luɔm (unofficial)	tiɛŋ luɔm	concubine
bëny (chief)	dït (big)	bënydït	senior chief, Lord God
pal (knife)	dït (big)	paldït	cutlass
raan (person)	dït (big)	raandït	an elder
jɔk (spirit)	rac (bad)	jɔŋrac	evil spirit

Compounds formed by combining nouns with verbs

Noun	Adjective	Compound	Gloss
raan (person)	piööc (teaching)	raanpiööc	teacher
kɔc (people)	piööcke (training)	kɔcpiööcke	disciples
moc (man)	thiëk (marrying)	monythiëk	bridegroom

The following are nouns plus verbs with the present simple tense marker /e/

raan (person)	e lim (he begs)	raan e lim	beggar
raan (person)	e thal (he cooks)	raan e thal	cook
γöt (house)	e thal	γön e thal	kitchen
kɔc (people)	e thäth (they forge metal)	kɔc e thäth	blacksmiths
kɔc (people)	kɔc e pur (cultivators)	kɔc e pur	cultivators
röör (men)	aye yïk (they thatch)	röör e yïk	thatchers
tuŋ (horn)	e cäm (used for eating)	tuŋ e cäm	spoon

4. 2. 1 Possessive morphemes in Dinka

(i) Examples of singular nouns joined with the singular possessive morphemes:

die (my)   du (your)   de (his, her, its)

rïŋ (meat)   rïŋdie (my meat)   rïŋde

weŋ (cow)   weŋdu (your cow)   weŋde

pɛɛm (chest)   pɛmde (his chest)   pɛmde

(ii) Singular nouns joined with plural possessive morphemes:

da (our)   dun (your, plural)   den (their)

Noun possessive morpheme   **Plural possessive morpheme**

Laŋ (neem tree)   laŋda (our neem tree)

thɔn (bull)   thɔndun (your bull)

töny (pot)   tönyden (their pot)

(iii) **Plural nouns joined with plural possessive morphemes**

kuɔ (our)   kun (your)   ken (their)

luëk (byres)   luëkkuɔ (our byres) luëkken

kueer (footpath)   kuɛrkuɔ (our footpaths)   kuɛrkun (your footpaths)

kuar (grandfathers)   kuarkun   kuarken

Similar examples:

Nyuɔɔcë në camdie (sit to my left)

laarë në ciindu (take it with your hand)

cɔk wec në cökke (let him kick it with his feet).

These examples show only singular possession as well as intimacy since *cam*, *cin* and *cök* are all parts of the body.

4.2.2.1   Demonstrative morpheme /ë/ (this)

Noun	Demonstrative morpheme	Gloss
yith (well)	yinhë	this well
wëër (dung)	wërë	this dung
waar (shoe)	waarë	this shoe
dhɔk	dhɔŋë	this boy
thööc (chair)	thönyë	this chair
kuur (stone)	kuurë	this stone

APPENDIX 47

4.2.2.2 Demonstrative morpheme tui (that)

tim (tree)	timtui	that tree
leŋ (drum)	leŋtui	that drum
dëël (grass tuft)	dëëltui	that tuft grass
raaan (person)	raantui	that person
tuɔŋ (egg)	tuɔŋtui	that egg
cɔɔr (blind person)	cɔɔrtui	that blind person
col (piece of charcoal)	coltui	that charcoal

4.2.2.3 Demonstrative morpheme "ke"

In these examples, "ke" will occur once as a suffix to plural nouns it may describe.

Noun	Plural demonstrative morpheme	Gloss
dëŋ (rains)	kedëŋkë	these rains
nyïïr (girls)	nyïïrkë	those girls
bëi (homesteads)	bëikë	those homesteads
bäny (chiefs)	bänykë	those chiefs
cök (feet)	cökkë	those feet
tuŋ (horns)	tuŋkë	those horns
läi (animals)	keläikë	these animals
kɔ̈ɔ̈r (lions)	keläikë	these lions
röör (men)	keröörkë	these men
kuëc (leopards)	kekuëckë	these leopards

4.2.2.4 Demonstrative morpheme "kui" (those)

Plural noun	Plural demonstrative morpheme	Gloss
nyïn (eyes)	nyïnkui	those eyes
rec (fishes)	reckui	those fishes
mëc (fires)	mëckui	those fires
rak (fences)	rakkui	those fences
Plural noun	**Plural demonstrative morpheme**	**Gloss**

tɔɔŋ (spears)   tɔɔŋkui   those spears

cöör (blind persons)   cöörkui   those blind persons

kur (stones)   kurkui   those stones

4.3.1 Cattle name prefix "a"

Adjectival colour	Cattle name prefix	Gloss
luɛl (red)	aluɛɛl	red cow
kɔ̈l (red with white)	akɔ̈l	red and white cow
këër (black and white)	akëër	black and white cow.

4.3.2 Cattle name with prefix "na"

Adjectival colour	Cattle name prefix	Gloss
lith (silver grey)	nalith	silver grey heifer
jök (black and white)	najök	black and white heifer
yäär (white)	nayäär	white heifer
thiëëŋ (dark brown)	nathiëŋ	dark brown heifer.

4.3.3. Cattle name prefix "ma"

Adjectival colour	Male cattle name prefix	Gloss

"Ma" is a cattle name prefix that refers to male cattle. The following are some of the examples:

bil (black and white belly)	mabil	bull with black and white belly
cäär (black)	macäär	black bull
këër (black and white back)	makëër	black and white back bull
yäär (white)	mayäär (mabiöör)	white bull
lɔu (ash-grey)	malɔu	ash-grey bull
bok (reddish grey)	mabok	reddish-grey bull
lual (red)	malual	red bull

APPENDIX

Reduplication

Like other languages of the world, Dinka uses replication of words to form meaningful morphemes or abstract nouns. The following illustrate this pattern:

Verb	Verb reduplicated	Gloss
rir (to mix)	rirrir	confusion
lɛŋ (to swing)	lɛŋlɛŋ	swinging
gɔ̈t (write-imperative)	gɔ̈tgɔ̈t	writing
kum (cover-imperative)	kumkum	coverage
rieth (cover- imperative)	riethrieth	slippery place
ŋuën (to hesitate)	ŋuëŋŋuën	hesitation

less than 200 miles south of Khartoum and just over 20 miles west of Sennar. According to Arkell, the excavation in Khartoum mentioned earlier revealed that:

> The early inhabitants were living on low sand-bank at the edge of the Blue Nile; they resembled the present day Nilotic peoples such as the Dinka of Bor District who camp on the edge of the Nile in situations where they are liable to be flooded at higher river, and largely live by spearing fish and harpooning hippopotamus.

However, the probable presence of African elements in the Pharaonic civilization is also evident in Shinnie (1967), based on thorough study of three skulls of Meroitic origin excavated in the tomb of King Amanitenmemide (45-47 CE). Two of these skulls were found to be persons of black race.

From all the above assertions, it can be deduced that the Nilotic people were among the black Africans who were known to be the Ancient Egyptians, Greek and Romans. They lived in the kingdoms of Kush and Meroe. They might have moved southward to Khartoum, Sennar, Kosti and further to where they live today. It is thus, undoubtedly acceptable that Dinka were included in the migration.

1.2 The name "Dinka" and its connotations

The word "Dinka" stands the name used by the people who are known by outsiders Dinka. The Dinka call themselves Jieeng or Jiëëŋ. "Dinka" is a recent coinage which dates back to the period during which the Dinka people first came into contact with Arab inhabitants probably between 15th – 16th centuries CE as stated by Hasan (1973).

www.ingramcontent.com/pod-product-compliance
Lightning Source LLC
Chambersburg PA
CBHW020331010526
44107CB00054B/2064